**EARTH UNDER ATTACK!**

# FOREST FIRE CREATES INFERNO

Louise and Richard Spilsbury

**Gareth Stevens**
PUBLISHING

Please visit our website, **www.garethstevens.com**.
For a free color catalog of all our high-quality books,
call toll free 1-800-542-2595 of fax 1-877-542-2596.

Cataloging-in-Publication Data
Names: Spilsbury, Louise. | Spilsbury, Richard.
Title: Forest fire creates inferno / Louise and Richard Spilsbury.
Description: New York : Gareth Stevens Publishing, 2018. | Series: Earth under attack! | Includes index.
Identifiers: ISBN 9781538213032 (pbk.) | ISBN 9781538213056 (library bound) | ISBN 9781538213049 (6 pack)
Subjects: LCSH: Forest fires--Juvenile literature. | Natural disasters--Juvenile literature.
Classification: LCC SD421.S67 2018 | DDC 634.9'618--dc23

First Edition

Published in 2018 by
**Gareth Stevens Publishing**
111 East 14th Street, Suite 349
New York, NY 10003

Copyright © 2018 Gareth Stevens Publishing

Produced for Gareth Stevens by Calcium
Editors: Sarah Eason and Jennifer Sanderson
Designers: Jeni Child and Simon Borrough
Picture researcher: Rachel Blount

Picture credits: Cover: Shutterstock: Anthony Heflin top, Lumppini bottom; Inside: Shutterstock: AAresTT 13, Africa Rising 6, Jeffrey B. Banke 24–25b, Alin Brotea 16, 21, Luciano Cosmo 8, David M G 30, De Visu 23, Stephen Denness 34, EcoPrint 11, Iakov Filimonov 12, Paula Fisher 19, Boris Florin 7, Halfofmoon 14–15, Mark Higgins 37, Humphery 41, Ingehogenbijl 45, Sarah Jessup 31, Kevin Key 24–25t, Kletr 43, Vladimir Melnikov 22, Mironov 18, Myszka 34–35t, NancyS 39, Peieq 26–27t, Polarpx 9, Ondrej Prosicky 44, Joseph Sohm 26, 40, Totajla 17, Valentyn Volkov 10, Wideweb 32, 33, Peter J. Wilson 5, You Touch Pix of EuToch 29, Andrii Zhezhera 38; Wikimedia Commons: Advanced Spaceborne Thermal Emission and Reflection Radiometer (ASTER) 44.

All rights reserved. No part of this book may be reproduced in any form without permission from the publisher, except by a reviewer.

Printed in China

CPSIA compliance information: Batch #Cw18GS:
For further information contact Gareth Stevens, New York, New York at 1-800-542-2595.

# CONTENTS

**CHAPTER 1**
Ferocious Fires .................................................. 4

**CHAPTER 2**
Ignition! ............................................................. 8

**CHAPTER 3**
Burning Conditions ......................................... 14

**CHAPTER 4**
Raging Firestorm ............................................ 20

**CHAPTER 5**
Fiery Battle ..................................................... 28

**CHAPTER 6**
Living with Fire ............................................... 36

**GLOSSARY** ........................................................ 46

**FOR MORE INFORMATION** ............................. 47

**INDEX** .............................................................. 48

## CHAPTER 1

# FEROCIOUS FIRES

Flames are a mesmerizing sight, as they flicker and dance on a lit candle. The heat and flames of a campfire are comforting on a dark night. Some fires, though, are terrifying and dangerous spectacles that blast burning heat all around. Enormous fires can start and consume buildings, but the biggest and most ferocious of all rage through forests and other wild areas.

## Wildfires

Wildfires are uncontrolled fires that burn in wild areas. The wildfires that happen in woodlands and forests are called forest fires. Those in areas of grassland and scrub, which is tough shrub plants, are often called bushfires. Peat fires are wildfires where peaty soil burns. Peat contains high quantities of the remains of dead plants that have not completely rotted.

## Burning Together

A forest fire starts among the trees. Once one tree is on fire, it warms the air around it and the surface of the trees next to it. Then, the warmed surrounding trees may catch fire, too. In some forests, there may be hundreds of thousands of trees, so vast areas can catch fire and burn at the same time. When the trees are burning together, they give off so much heat that other trees burn faster and faster. The fire can be passed along between trees via smaller plants growing in woodland spaces, too. This means that the fire can spread through a forest even if the trees are not close together. Fire spreads quicker if the trees are dry, which is usually in drier, warmer seasons of the year and in places with dry **climates**.

> Forest fires are incredibly destructive and deadly forces of change that rage through the world's woodlands.

**EARTH UNDER ATTACK!** Globally, an area of forest approximately equivalent to the size of New Zealand burns each year. That is 1 percent of the world's forest cover, which in turn covers about one-third of the land on our planet.

# Scorched Earth

**Fires can be catastrophic—not only for the trees in a forest, but also for the people and other animals that live there. Some animals, such as birds and deer, may be able to fly from or outrun the flames, but others, such as snakes and livestock kept in fields, may be burned alive.**

A forest fire can ignite trees so fast that firefighters may sometimes struggle to halt its spread.

## Fire Attack

Fires can devastate human communities living in or near forests. The flames do not restrict themselves to trees but burn many other materials, too. These include wooden boards, beams of houses and other buildings, plastics in cars, and other objects. A fire's intense heat buckles metal sheets, bridges, telegraph poles, and railroad tracks. It can melt asphalt from roads, too. Fires keep burning so long as there are materials that can burn. They can move quickly, too, especially if the wind fans them. Some forest fires can move at 14 miles per hour (23 km/h), which is the speed of a marathon runner. They can leap hundreds of feet when burning sparks blow off a fire and set fire to trees where they land.

## Blackened Landscape

After the flames of a forest fire have been extinguished, a blackened landscape is left behind. Many charred tree trunks are still standing, but the earth between the trees is often piled up with charred wood and dusty ash. These may remain searingly hot, just like the ash and burned wood in a campfire. It is difficult to breathe during and after a forest fire because of the amount of choking smoke in the air.

### DEADLY DATA

The yard-high flames of a small forest fire can reach temperatures of 1,472° Fahrenheit (800° C) or more. That is twice as hot as an average pizza oven. In a tall forest, flames can reach 150 feet (50 m) high and 2,192° Fahrenheit (1,200° C). That is nearly a quarter of the temperature of the surface of the sun.

After a forest fire burned it down, all that has been left behind of this home in Russia is the fireplace and chimney stack, plus some roofing materials and bricks.

### CHAPTER 2

# IGNITION!

However big a forest fire is, it always starts with part of a tree being heated to a temperature at which it will burst into flames. We say that something has "ignited" when it starts to burn. But how does fire happen?

## Reaction

Some people think of a **chemical reaction** as something that happens in an experiment in a laboratory, when something changes color or fizzes. However, burning is a common chemical reaction, too. In this reaction, a gas called oxygen, which is found in air, combines with a substance that can burn, called a **fuel**. In a forest fire, the fuel includes wood, bark, leaves, roots, and other parts of trees. This reaction can happen only when there is heat to drive it onward.

## Fire Triangle

No fire can happen unless it has oxygen, heat, and fuel. These fire ingredients are like the corners of a fire triangle. A large forest fire uses a lot of all three ingredients. For example, in a forest fire in 1987 in China, a vast area of forest burned in a moving wall of flames. The wall moved so quickly that it sucked most of the oxygen from the air ahead of it. The firefighters' truck engines stopped working because there was not enough oxygen in the air to burn the diesel fuel, so they struggled to fight the fire.

Fire is a chemical reaction that needs heat, fuel, and oxygen.

The heat that starts many forest fires comes from lightning strikes. For example, in Canada, lightning causes 45 percent of all forest fires.

**EARTH UNDER ATTACK!**

The temperature at which wood catches fire is 572° Fahrenheit (300° C). This is called its flash point. At this temperature, wood releases gases that react with oxygen, which produces flames. During the burning reaction, the fuel changes as oxygen combines with it. Wood, for example, changes from a strong, solid fibrous material to crumbly, black charred wood and soft ash. The reaction also releases heat. This heat raises more wood to its flash point, so the fire spreads.

# Causes of Forest Fires

There are many causes of the initial ignition that starts a forest fire. They can be natural, but most forest fires are the result of human activity.

## Natural Causes

Some forest fires are started by lightning strikes. The heat in a bolt of lightning is caused by energy stored in clouds when hailstones bash and rub together. Others are naturally caused by volcanoes. These are holes in Earth where red-hot melted rock called lava from deep underground comes to the surface. Lava is usually 1,300 to 2,200° Fahrenheit (700 to 1,200° C). Sometimes, volcanoes erupt without lava flow and produce searingly hot clouds of ash instead. Hot lava and ash can easily set trees on fire and start forest fires. Occasionally, fires can start after rocks fall and produce sparks when they strike other rocks. Rarely, piles of hay, manure, coal, and other materials can become hot enough to ignite without the need for a spark.

Sparks from the leaping flames of a bonfire can start a forest fire. Sticks or leaves that stay hot after people leave a campsite often catch fire.

## Human Causes

People cause around 80 percent of forest fires. Some of these are intentional. Many are the result of slash-and-burn farming. Farmers cut down forest, often using chain saws, and then light small fires to clear the land of the remaining stumps and waste wood. They do this so that they can plant crops or keep livestock there. These fires then spread to surrounding forest. Others fires are accidental. For example, power lines and electrical machinery can produce sparks that act like mini lightning bolts and start fires. Other human causes include campfires that people do not put out completely when they leave a forest, or smoldering cigarette butts that people may throw on the ground. Arsonists are criminals who start fires, including forest fires, just to cause damage.

Slash-and-burn farmers have cleared a space in a woodland area in Mozambique, Southern Africa, without harming the surrounding trees. Many such farmers are not so careful.

### DEADLY DATA

In Indonesia in 2015, slash-and-burn farmers started more than 100,000 forest fires. The fires destroyed rainforests and killed rare animals, such as orangutans. The enormous amount of smoke stretched across Indonesia, Singapore, and Malaysia, causing serious breathing difficulties for around half a million people.

# Disaster Report: 2010, Russia

In 2010, Russia was experiencing the hottest summer in its history. At first, Russians enjoyed the heat after yet another bitter winter. But soon, people were trying mightily to stay cool. Then, the high temperatures started hundreds of fires across the country. Russia was on fire and the skies turned dark with smoke.

## Fire Raising

The average maximum July temperature for Moscow, the capital of Russia, is around 73° Fahrenheit (23° C). In 2010, however, some regions of the country were sweltering under temperatures that hit 111° Fahrenheit (44° C). Every year in Russia, some small forest fires start accidentally in the county's dense woodlands, especially when the trees are unusually dry. That summer, the high temperatures combined with a severe **drought** and strong winds, which whipped up and raised small fires to dangerous infernos.

The **atmosphere** in and around the city of Vladimir, like many others in Russia in 2010, was heavily polluted with smoke.

In 2010, walls of flames were out of control across Russia, blocked only by features such as this canal.

## Country Ablaze

That summer through fall, around 600 large fires blazed in Russia. They destroyed at least 2,000 homes and spread dangerously close to major towns and cities, including Moscow. The firestorm burned around 3,000 square miles (7,770 sq km), which is just a little less than the area of Crete in Greece. A third of Russia's grain fields were turned to ashes. More than 200,000 firefighters, 30,000 trucks and fire engines, and about 200 aircraft struggled to fight the fires.

The choking smoke from the fires was a major health hazard. It cloaked Moscow for weeks, even seeping into underground subway stations. The smoke made people choke and cough, gave them watery eyes, and caused serious breathing problems. The smoke trapped the citizens of Moscow indoors, leaving the streets empty and the schools closed. The city ground to a halt. Flights had to be canceled due to the poor air visibility.

### DEADLY DATA

The Russian government said that the fires killed 65 people and injured more than 1,000. However, unofficially, the figures were much higher. For example, death rates doubled in Moscow as a result of illnesses caused and made worse by the dangerous smoke **pollution**.

13

# CHAPTER 3
# BURNING CONDITIONS

One corner of the fire triangle is fuel, and it is obvious that forest fires can happen only where there are many trees as fuel. Forests range from small plantations to mighty forests as far as the eye can see, and these can contain very different communities of trees. Forest fires can happen in any type of forest.

## Forest Types

The largest forest type, boreal forest, grows in the cold, windy, and dark regions south of the Arctic. This is mostly in Alaska, Canada, Scandinavia, and Siberia. Typical trees here include firs, spruces, and pines, with small needle-shaped leaves and cones. These are types of coniferous trees. Tropical forests grow in areas of Africa, South America, and Southeast Asia near the equator. Here, there are high temperatures and high rainfall all year round, with generally moist conditions. The temperate forests of the eastern United States, Western Europe, and parts of Asia are dominated by deciduous trees. These include oak and beech, which drop their old leaves to the ground in fall to avoid leaf damage in cold winters. New leaves regrow in warm springs and summers. The final forest type is Mediterranean and is found in southern Europe, North Africa, and Australia. Here, there are long, hot, and dry summers and short, damp winters. Forest fires happen mostly in the drier, warmest seasons in any forest type.

This is a mixed forest in the fall with some evergreen conifers and many deciduous trees with colorful fall leaves.

## Fire Season

Different countries and different parts of countries experience the worst conditions for forest fires at different times of year. This is the result of a region's climate. For example, in India, the typical fire season is from January to June. After this, there are heavy **monsoon** rains. They put out fires, but they also cause widespread flooding. California has two fire seasons. The Santa Ana season is in fall, when hot, dry winds blow from inland areas toward the coast, spreading fires quickly. The summer season is when summer sun dries and heats forests up, so they are ready to burn.

### EARTH UNDER ATTACK!

Some rainforest trees encourage forest fires. Eucalyptus trees have rubbery leaves filled with oils that burn easily. When fires happen, the leaves and ragged, light bark catch on fire, but the trunks usually survive. Burning bark fragments blow onto and ignite other trees, too. Eucalyptus trees grow fast from seeds on the cleared land after a fire.

# Air and Fire

People can start campfires or home fires by blowing air onto the first piece of fuel to catch fire, often using bellows. This increases the flow of oxygen over more of the fuel, which spreads the burning reaction and makes the fire grow. Wind speeds up forest fires in the same way.

The wind is blowing from right to left, pushing the flames of this natural fire at an angle. The heat of the flames then ignites more and more plants.

## Winds

Winds not only speed the horizontal movement of fires, but moving air also **evaporates** water from the surface of fuel, so it dries out and ignites more easily. Wind direction determines which way a fire will spread through a forest. Forest fires can also create their own winds. Air above a fire is heated and then rises into the atmosphere. This reduces the air pressure, or push from air, by the fire. Then, colder, higher pressure air moves into the gap.

This creates fire-generated winds that blow toward the fire up to ten times faster than the surrounding wind speeds. Sometimes, these winds can become so fast that they produce incredibly quick **forward bursts** of flames, when fire accelerates through the trees at the speed of a flamethrower. Violent, fire-generated winds can blow the flames hundreds of feet upward in a spinning **fire whirl**.

## Moisture

When it is time to go indoors and a campfire is no longer needed, people often stop the flames by pouring water over them. Rainfall or snowstorms can cool and douse forest fires, too. Very **humid** air can dampen trees, branches, and other woody **debris** on a forest floor, so they take much longer to ignite. Similarly, when there are drought conditions with unusually low rainfall, fires will have lots of dry fuel to burn.

### DEADLY DATA

Fire whirls in forest fires can move at speeds of 100 miles per hour (161 km/hour) and reach heights of 300 feet (91 m).

Fire whirls draw smoke and flame up fast, high above the burning ground.

# Fueling the Fire

**Once a forest fire begins to burn, it can either fizzle out or grow into a raging blaze, depending in part on what fuel is available.**

## Best Burners

Some types of tree burn better than others. Coniferous trees generally burn faster than deciduous trees. The reason is that coniferous trees have a lot of sticky sap, or resin, in their branches. The resin evaporates into highly flammable gases, which supply a lot of heat for ignition of the wood. Usually, coniferous trees also grow more closely together than deciduous trees, so fires in deciduous forests can spread more easily.

This advancing fire front is moving to the right, leaving smoking, smoldering trees, and ground cover it has burned in its wake.

Peat soil is a concentrated **fuel load** that natural fires burn easily. After a surface fire is put out, deep peat can remain smoldering many feet underground, ready to burst into flames again if air reaches it.

## Fuel Load

The amount of fuel per area of ground surrounding a fire is called the fuel load. Forests burn more slowly if there is a smaller fuel load than if the fuel load is larger. However, the amount of fuel is not the only thing that affects burning. Compared with a twig, a giant tree has a larger **surface area** where the burning reaction can occur. However, it burns much slower than a twig because it has a much higher volume. The thick wood needs more time to heat up to ignition temperature than the thin twig. Twigs, dry grass, dry leaves, dry cones, and pine needles are called **flashy fuels** because they burst into flames fast and easily. Not all the fuel load is above ground. Roots, dead wood debris, and peat soil burn well, too. Fires can slow or even stop when they reach places with no fuel load, such as rivers and wide roads.

### EARTH UNDER ATTACK!

The slope of the land also affects forest fires. Fires usually travel uphill much faster than downhill. The reason is that, on slopes, trees may be growing slightly closer together, and winds also tend to blow up hills. This is because air pressure at higher altitudes is generally lower than air pressure at ground level, and air blows from high- to low-pressure areas. Heat rises, so it dries and warms the trees ahead of the fire faster than on horizontal ground.

## CHAPTER 4

# RAGING FIRESTORM

**The raging firestorm of a big forest fire can move very fast. Often, people do not know about the firestorm until it descends. However, there are warning signs that can help people evacuate to places of safety.**

### Fire Signs

Sometimes, it is possible to see rising smoke and flames from a distant section of forest, but people among the trees often have their view obstructed. One of the first signs on the ground is a faint smell of wood smoke. A glance at any cars, tents, or roofs of buildings might reveal a dusting of ash. The sky might look hazy, too. Thickening smoke and increasing ashfall are signs of the fire getting closer, along with sounds. Large fires are noisy with the sounds of crackling wood, falling trees, and squeaks and pops when gases escape from hot wood. Once it gets windier, as air is sucked toward the fire, the fire has almost arrived.

### Moving Forward

Not all forest fires advance as a solid wall of flame. Surface fires spread through flashy fuels on the ground and set trees on fire from the ground up. The process is helped by smaller plants growing among the trees. For example, climbing plants, such as vines and ivy, grow tall by clinging onto tree trunks. Fire can ignite their thin stems, burn upward, and then set fire to the leafy part of the tree higher up, called the crown. Crown fires spread faster through a forest. These fires rage up high, with intense heat passing from crown to crown. Some leap large distances from a burning crown when fast-rising winds blow burning embers, known as fireballs, high into the air. The fireballs may start crown fires in new places where they land. This process is called fire spotting.

## DEADLY DATA

Fireballs can keep burning for up to 6 minutes in the air. They can travel for thousands of feet before they land and start new fires.

A crown fire rages through a coniferous forest. The upward draft of hot air has produced a natural flamethrower.

# Fire Dangers

**One of the reasons that forest fires are so terrifying is because they are so hazardous to people and animals. They can cause anything from minor injuries to life-threatening, serious illnesses, and even death.**

## Burns

The high air temperatures and flames of a forest fire can singe, scald, and redden skin on the surface, and can also cause extensive burns over the entire body. The skin is the largest organ on the human body. It is there to protect our insides from external dangers and to form a waterproof layer. When skin is badly burned, **bacteria** can enter the body, causing sicknesses that require careful medical attention. Burns can also form scars that are not flexible like regular skin, making activities such as moving arms and breathing more difficult for burn victims.

> Smoke from a big forest fire rises and spreads far and wide through the atmosphere.

*People wear masks to try to prevent breathing in particulate matter and harmful gases from forest fires.*

## Smoke Hazard

The most widespread impact of forest fires on health is caused by smoke. The sheer volume of burning fuel load fills the air with smoke. This irritates eyes, so they redden and start streaming. When people breathe in smoke, it makes them cough and can cause damage to their lungs. Smoke contains poisonous gases, such as mercury vapor and carbon monoxide. These form when wood and leaves in the fuel load smolder, rather than burn with a flame.

Smoke also contains particulate matter, which is extremely tiny, jagged particles of unburned material. When people breathe in these, the particles get trapped deep inside their lungs. Particulate matter can cause breathing difficulties especially in young and elderly people, and also those with existing conditions such as **asthma**. The tiniest particles can even burrow out from the lungs and damage other organs, such as the heart.

### DEADLY DATA

Each year, wildfires, including forest fires, release around 2 million tons (1.8 mt) of particulate matter into Earth's atmosphere. This is more than the amount that comes from polluting vehicles and factories.

23

# Meltdown

**Forest fires cause widespread damage and destruction. For many animals in the forest, fire destroys the habitat they live in and their sources of food, including the leaves and nuts on trees. Some forest animals, such as orangutans, tree kangaroos, and forest elephants, are now increasingly endangered because of habitat loss caused partly by forest fires.**

## Fire Damage

Forest fires transform human habitats. The flames quickly burn down homes, schools, and other buildings. They can melt asphalt, ruining roads and playgrounds, and bend metal structures. Flaming branches can fall onto and burn through power lines, causing electrical failure and **electrocution** hazards. Fire can ignite gas at fuel depots and gas stations, and in canisters and pipes in homes, causing dangerous explosions. The heat can melt or shatter glass, turn vinyl gutters and downspouts into a gooey mess, and even damage some types of concrete. When the concrete used to hold together bricks crumbles in a fire, whole walls can fall down. The smoke from forest fires can seep into buildings and make everything smell of smoke long after the fire has been extinguished.

Intense heat from a forest fire in California has burned cars, leaving behind metal shells.

## Damaging the Land

Forest fires cause damage to soils, too. Forest soils are rich in nutrients that help trees and other plants grow. They are home to bacteria, fungi, wood lice, and other living things that help break down, or decay, debris to release the nutrients. Intense heat can destroy these communities as they burn up the soil. With fewer nutrients, some plants struggle to grow on treeless land. Fires can damage some soils, so that they are less able to retain water. Then water runs off the surface when it rains, sometimes causing floods. However, loss of tree cover from slopes after a forest fire can also make soil unstable. Tree roots usually stop soil from sliding downhill. After a fire has cleared trees, heavy rains can wash soil from slopes to become **landslides**, which can cause great damage to settlements.

The stone shell and metal fence posts are all that remain of a beautiful woodland home after a forest fire.

### EARTH UNDER ATTACK!

In Indonesia, forest is regularly burned to clear land for agriculture. When their natural habitat burns away in forest fires, tigers and elephants may stray onto plantations and also into villages. People then sometimes trap or kill the animals because they fear for their safety or are trying to protect their crops.

# Disaster Report: 2016, California, USA

Between May and September 2016, a massive sequence of wildfires raged across California. An intense summer fire season had been predicted by weather experts, but no one expected quite as much land to be on fire.

## Weather for Fire

California had suffered droughtlike conditions for years before this damaging fire season. These conditions were caused by unusually low amounts of rainfall. Rain in California normally happens when moist air over the Pacific Ocean blows inland. The moist air rises over the Sierra Nevada Mountains, cools, and condenses into rainfall. However, changing wind patterns stopped the moist air from reaching the land. The land became a giant tinderbox, and during the fire season, nearly 7,000 wildfires burned.

*The hills were on fire with the smell of smoke in and around Hollywood in 2016.*

On July 23, 2016, a wildfire called the Sand Fire engulfs the northeast side of a freeway in Santa Clarita, California.

## Blue Cut

One of the worst fires started midmorning on August 16, 2016, north of San Bernardino near the Blue Cut mountain hiking trail. Winds funneled through the nearby Cajon Pass and blew embers as far as half a mile (0.8 km) away, producing many spotting fires. Within a day, the fires had consumed 46 square miles (119 sq km).

Residents in the area scrambled to grab possessions and move away from the advancing fire. The governor of California declared a state of emergency, and agencies ordered the evacuation of more than 80,000 people. Many homes and businesses were burned down, including a famous diner on the Route 66 highway. More than 1,000 firefighters, 15 helicopters, and 10 air tankers carrying water worked to contain the fire. One tactic firefighters used was to dig trenches in gaps in the forest to remove a band of fuel load. However, the wind-whipped flames leaped into the gaps! There was even a terrifying fire whirl shooting flames tens of feet high, right at the edge of the main interstate. Officials closed this route between Los Angeles and Las Vegas because of the smoke and flames.

### DEADLY DATA

The 2016 California wildfire season killed seven people and burned nearly 888 square miles (2,300 sq km), including the hills surrounding the famous Los Angeles suburb of Hollywood, famous for its movie industry.

## CHAPTER 5

# FIERY BATTLE

As soon as a forest fire starts, a team of trained and brave firefighters springs into action. Fires spread quickly, so firefighters have to reach the fire and start battling the flames as soon as they can. They use different ways to fight forest fires, but the aim of all these methods is to deprive the fire of one of the three things it needs to grow: fuel, oxygen, or heat.

## Firefighters at Work

Some forest firefighters work from fire engines that carry special equipment to spray water and foam onto flames. Spraying water onto a fire makes the wood too wet to burn, and it can suppress oxygen to the flames, removing two of the elements that a fire needs. Sometimes, tankers bring water to fire engines, or firefighters set up pumps to feed their hoses from a water source near the fire. Firefighters also use bulldozers, axes, rakes, and other equipment to remove trees and dig up plants that the fire could use as fuel to help it spread.

## Firebreaks

The firefighters' main objective is to clear a firebreak, or fire line. This is a strip of land or a ring around the fire where there are no dry plants or debris that the fire can use as fuel to continue its onward blaze. Firefighters carefully set the fuel load on fire, or they use bulldozers to clear the ground between this boundary and the advancing fire. When the fire reaches this point, it has nothing to feed on, so it should die out. Firefighters may use a natural boundary, such as a road or stream, as a firebreak, too.

This powerful helicopter is called a SkyCrane. It is used here to suck up, carry, and deliver heavy loads of liquids to put out forest fires.

## EARTH UNDER ATTACK!

Firefighters are at great risk from burning or being choked by smoke when they are called to a wildfire. They wear oxygen masks to help them breathe and clothing made from a fireproof material to protect them from the intense heat. Sometimes, they carry special tents called fire shelters, which can protect them if they become trapped by forest fires.

# Attack from Above

**When a wildfire strikes in a remote location or spreads too far and wide to be controlled by firefighters on the ground alone, the flames must be attacked from above. Helicopters and airplanes transport firefighters and firefighting equipment quickly to the heart of the fire action.**

> Aerial firefighters try to reduce the intensity of a wildfire or the speed at which it spreads, so that ground firefighters can create a firebreak.

## Firefighters in the Sky

Special aircraft called air tankers are deployed to fly over a fire. They dump large quantities of water or fire retardant onto a blaze. Fire retardants are chemicals that slow or stop things from burning. Just like water, they cool them and block oxygen. They also cling to and form a protective layer on trees, which stops the burning reaction. Fire retardants include "sky jello," a pink substance that can smother flames instantly. Sometimes, a plane will carry a giant container of water suspended below it that it pours over the fire. Helicopters dump water, too, and can then hover over lakes to refill their vast buckets. In some places, firefighters use drones, or unmanned robots that are controlled by computers, to survey an area of fire. They may use unmanned air tankers to drop fire retardant. This allows firefighters to keep their distance and avoid putting their lives at risk.

Parachuting right into the action, smoke jumpers must be ready for the hard work of fighting fires in difficult settings.

## Smoke Jumpers

Some elite forest firefighters are known as smoke jumpers. Smoke jumpers jump out of aircraft and parachute to the ground near a fire. Firefighting tools, food, and water are dropped by parachute to the smoke jumpers after they land. To keep smoke jumpers safe while they are trying to control the fire, crew on helicopters hovering above use walkie-talkies to tell them if the wind direction changes and the fire changes direction, for example.

### DEADLY DATA

The Boeing 747-400 Global SuperTanker can carry 19,200 gallons (72,680 L) of fire retardant and travel almost 600 miles per hour (966 km/h).

# After the Flames

After the flames have died down, people start to help those affected by a forest fire. The priority is making them safe and providing basic needs, such as shelter and food. Then, the process of rebuilding survivors' lives can begin.

## Rescue!

Firefighters rescue victims caught up in a blaze, sometimes using helicopters to airlift them from the flames. After fires are under control, disaster response teams arrive to help victims who were injured in the fire. They perform emergency first aid and transport the seriously burned and injured to nearby hospitals. Aid workers may set up temporary accommodation, such as tents or in public buildings, give out food and drinking water, and help survivors locate missing or injured friends and family members. Some workers rescue and treat injured animals, too.

*Aid workers register and take care of people who evacuated a forest fire near Haifa, Israel, in 2016.*

## Cleaning Up

Workers have to clear piles of debris from broken buildings and burned-out cars, for example, and clean up large amounts of ash. They must do this with caution while wearing safety gloves and other safety equipment, such as breathing masks. That is because piles of debris may be hot, unstable, or contain sharp edges or nails that can cause harm. Disturbing ash on the ground can send it airborne in choking clouds; it can also reveal smoldering wood that could catch fire again in a gust of wind. Workers soak the ground to stabilize ash and cool smoldering debris. Electrical equipment may start fires if damaged and near water, so they must all be checked before power supplies can be turned back on.

> Exhausted firefighters may need to wear special equipment to tackle further blazes in different areas before one forest fire is even put out.

**EARTH UNDER ATTACK!**

Fire retardants often contain chemicals similar to fertilizers. These chemicals run off from land into streams and rivers when rain falls on burned land. They can affect water quality, so it can make people sick if they drink it and can also harm animals. For example, ammonia from retardants harms salmon and their young in rivers.

# Disaster Report:
## 2009, Black Saturday Fire, Victoria, Australia

The ferocious bushfires that swept through the state of Victoria in Australia on Saturday, February 2, 2009, were the most devastating in Australian history. The fires were so terrifying and damaging that the day that they started is known as "Black Saturday."

### Tinderbox

It had been a hot summer, and the week before the fires, thermometers had reached record-breaking February temperatures of 115.5° Fahrenheit (46.4° C) in the Victoria area. This heat wave had caused a drought that dried up a lot of plants in the area. Then, on February 7, fast, hot winds blew down power lines, and sparks ignited the first fire. As the day progressed, the fire increased and was spread quickly by winds that blew huge fireballs through the trees and towns. Other fires began, and by evening, there were almost 400 individual blazes across the state.

Black Saturday burned forest fast and furiously through Victoria, as far as the eye could see.

It took just one day for the fire to devastate settlements and communities established over hundreds of years.

## Fighting the Fires

Firefighters faced terrible challenges. The fires created winds of 75 miles per hour (120 km/h), columns of smoke thousands of feet high, flames that leaped 60 feet (100 m) into the air, and a noise like hundreds of jet engines all rumbling together. Firefighters had to travel through roads riddled with debris and burned-out cars that had been involved in multiple collisions. They used **controlled burning** and chain saws to clear trees and create firebreaks, and also pumps to spray flames with water. One of the people who died in the fires was a 47-year-old firefighter who was crushed by a falling tree. Some fires merged, and in spite of the best efforts of almost 20,000 firefighters, the burning continued for days. Only a change in the weather helped the firefighters extinguish the fires.

### DEADLY DATA

In total, the forest fires that struck Victoria in 2009 killed 173 people, injured 414 others, and destroyed 2,000 homes. More than a million wild and farm or pet animals died, and 1,111,974 acres (450,000 ha) of land were burned.

## CHAPTER 6

# LIVING WITH FIRE

**Forest fires are terrifying, destructive phenomena. However, fire also has its benefits for the health of forests and for people who rely on forests, too.**

## Natural Benefits

Like any living thing, trees have a certain life span. It is vital for a species to produce young that can replace individual trees once they die. Trees produce seeds that sprout into seedlings, which grow into saplings and then adult trees. Some species, such as *Banksia* and scrub oak, need fire to reproduce. The intense heat from forest fires makes their tough, fireproof seedcases open. Then, the seeds fall out and can sprout in the cleared soil. Some species even encourage fire by having resin-covered leaves that catch on fire easily.

Small fires burn low plants and spindly, weak trees in forests. With fewer small or weak plants, there can be more nutrients in the soil for large, healthy trees to flourish. Large forest fires may not take hold if there are fewer small trees. Ash from burned trees can supply nutrients to nourish remaining trees, too. Diseases caused by viruses and fungi that insects spread are major forest killers. Some insect pests breed and increase in numbers in dead trees. Fire kills these disease causers and spreaders, stopping them from spreading to healthy areas of forest.

Grass trees burned to stumps by a fire in Australia sprouted new leaves just 2 weeks later. Fast regrowth increases the trees' chance of growing and producing seeds in the forest gaps caused by fire.

## Controlled Fires

Foresters and people living in forests encourage the natural benefits of fire by setting trees on fire. Controlled burns are when people set fire to particular areas of forest. They often use devices called drip burners, which drip and ignite fuel such as diesel, or special flares called fuses to start fires. The plants that shoot up in burned areas are often richer in nutrients and tastier than dead debris and old plants, so burned areas are good for grazing livestock. Cleared areas also provide better, more open habitat for some endangered species, such as Florida panthers.

**EARTH UNDER ATTACK!**

Some animals benefit from fire, too. Fire-chaser beetles seek out fire. They have special pits by their legs to detect heat from a forest fire tens of miles away. These beetles move to the fire site to mate and for females to lay eggs in soft, fire-damaged trunks.

# Preventing Fire

**People can help prevent fires or lessen their spread by reducing fuel load and making their properties less likely to burn. The time and cost spent on prevention is usually less than that needed to deal with big blazes.**

## Fire with Fire

One way to help prevent future forest fires is to let small fires burn. Controlled burns are often used to create firebreaks, for example, near settlements or roads. Another way to stop big fires is to let small natural forest fires burn if they are not harming anyone. When firefighters put out every fire, dead trees, small plants, and debris build up in large fuel loads over time, ready to burn longer and more ferociously when a large fire hits.

## Forest Management

An important part of fire prevention is the management of forests. People can cut dead branches from trees, since these contain drier wood that ignites more easily than healthy, moister wood. People can also increase the spaces between tree crowns by thinning overlapping branches and removing branches and any climbers within 13 feet (4.5 m) of ground level. This can help prevent the spread of crown and ground-to-crown fires.

Firebreaks, such as this one dug into soil next to a forest stand, are frontline defenses against spreading fire.

## Fireproof Homes

People can also reduce damage from forest fires by making them less likely to burn. For example, they can spray wooden structures with fire-resistant sprays and plant tree species such as oaks, rather than coniferous trees, around their properties. These are less likely to burn and spread fires toward their homes. Homeowners can help firefighters who try to protect properties from fire by providing a source of water to douse the flames, such as a cistern filled with rainwater or a swimming pool.

### DEADLY DATA

A devastating fire in Chile killed 11 people, burned 2,000 square miles (5,180 sq km) of land, and devastated settlements partly because people had planted a lot of eucalyptus trees close together on plantations. These oil-rich trees burn and spread fire easily. Also, there were far too few firebreaks to control the spread of the fire.

Workers convert fallen branches and flashy fuels left over winter into wood chips to help reduce fuel load for summer forest fires.

# Preparing for Fires

**In many places and at particular times of the year, forest fires are predictable and inevitable. So how do people prepare for them?**

## Fire Warnings

People keep track of warnings about potential fires. They listen to radio, television, and Internet broadcasts warning of weather conditions suitable for fire, such as high temperatures, low humidity, and high winds. Meteorologists and forestry agencies collect data on weather and also conditions on the ground in forests. Governments use this information to produce warnings about fire weather, for example, through the National Weather Service. In the United States, a Fire Weather Watch means that there is the potential for severe fire weather in the coming 12 to 24 hours. However, a Red Flag Warning indicates the imminent danger of severe fire weather.

Smoky the Bear signs in the United States warn people of the risk of forest fires.

Firefighters visit schools to give lessons on what to do if a fire occurs. They teach students how to use fire extinguishers and tools, such as beaters, to stop flames.

## Be Prepared

People living in or near forests plan for a worst-case scenario by putting together a disaster supply kit. This includes items such as a radio to hear fire news, food, water, a first-aid kit, and breathing masks. Families also have an emergency plan. They plan how to escape from their home if it catches fire and evacuation routes to safe places, such as playing fields or coastlines. They agree on places to meet or ways to communicate if they are separated when a fire hits. If an evacuation order is given, people have a plan, for example, to put pets, valuable documents, and photos in the car, ready to go, and for turning off the gas supply to their house.

**EARTH UNDER ATTACK!**

When fire is threatening them, people should know what to do to survive. For example, if your clothes catch fire, "Stop, Drop, and Roll." This means stop moving to prevent fanning the flames, drop to the ground, and roll around to keep oxygen from getting to the flames!

# Early Warning

The earlier a forest fire can be spotted, the less damage it may cause. It is easier to fight smaller fires than larger fires, and it is easier to prepare for a fire if there is more time. For this reason, early warning systems are a vital weapon against fires.

This image was produced on a **satellite** in space using data from a **sensor** that can detect heat and smoke near the ground.

## On the Ground

Each year, some forest fires are reported by visitors to woodlands, but such sightings are fairly random. That is why there are fire lookout towers spread through the world's forests. These tall structures allow people to see over the forest to spot fire signs, such as smoke. However, many towers are equipped with instruments that detect signs of fire automatically, without people. Webcams transmit images to control centers for people to look for fire signs. Some sensors on towers detect **infrared radiation**, which is produced when things heat up and burn. Others detect humidity or the changing clarity of air caused by smoke.

Quadcopters like this are stable aerial platforms for cameras and scientific instruments used to monitor and better understand forest fires.

## In the Sky

Early fire warnings also come from much higher up than lookout towers. Airplanes, helicopters, and drones fly over forests, especially during fire seasons. They have infrared cameras on board that take photos at particular locations regularly, controlled by **GPS** systems. These operate like the GPS in cars to calculate exact positions on Earth by comparing them with the fixed location of a satellite in space. By comparing consecutive photos, computer programs can identify changes in heat produced from forests. Forest fires can also be seen using infrared sensors on weather satellites in space.

### EARTH UNDER ATTACK!

An infrared sensor called VIIRS, which has been in space since 2015, can detect hot areas of forest with a spatial resolution of 1,230 feet (375 m). This is a measure of how accurate it can pinpoint a fire's location and size. Previous sensors had spatial resolutions of up to 7.5 miles (12 km), so they were not good at spotting fires until they were too big to control easily.

# Future Forest Fires

> People should respect the dangers of forest fires and behave in ways that prevent uncontrolled blazes.

**Forest fires are incredible forces of nature that will continue into the future. They will happen wherever the dangerous combination of warm, dry, windy conditions and high fuel load occur in forests. However, their frequency and strength could change as a result of global warming.**

## Changing Atmosphere

Most scientists agree that Earth's atmosphere is getting warmer. This is happening because human activities, such as burning fuels in power plants, are creating more gases such as carbon dioxide that stay in the atmosphere. The gases store heat from the sun, so the planet gets warmer very gradually. This global warming is causing **climate change** by altering weather patterns around the globe, such as making warm areas cooler and humid areas drier. Meteorologists are already noticing longer droughts in some places and more forest fires. For example, California's fire season has extended by 78 days since the 1970s, due to drier winters, warmer springs, and hotter summers.

## Living with Forests

Forests are beautiful places that supply valuable timber resources, homes for wildlife, and places for human recreation. Tree roots and forest soils store and filter freshwater many animals need to survive. It is vital that people look after forests by developing better fire control, prevention and detection methods, while understanding the natural benefits of fire for trees and forest communities.

**EARTH UNDER ATTACK!**

Forest fires are also increasing in frequency due to **feedback** between forests and the atmosphere. Like other plants, trees take in carbon dioxide to make food by photosynthesis. With fewer trees as a result of forest fires, less carbon dioxide is removed from the atmosphere, so it builds up and stores more heat. Forest fires release carbon dioxide when wood burns, which adds to global warming, making forest fire conditions more likely.

Forest fires provide opportunities for some species, such as these resprouting trees, but terrifying and rapid change for many others.

# GLOSSARY

**asthma** a medical condition that makes breathing difficult

**atmosphere** a blanket of gases that surrounds a planet

**bacteria** tiny living things that cause disease and also help break down waste

**chemical reaction** a process where several substances combine and change into other substances

**climate change** a change in weather patterns and rise in extreme weather events, for example, caused by global warming

**climates** the usual patterns of weather that happen in places

**controlled burning** setting fire to a particular area of land

**debris** fallen branches, twigs, leaves, seeds, and rotting trunks

**drought** a period of unusually dry weather with extremely low levels of rainfall

**electrocution** injury or death caused by electricity as it passes through someone's body

**evaporates** turns from a liquid into a gas

**feedback** when something produced by a system changes what that system produces. For example, burning trees make global warming worse, and that causes more forest fires.

**fire whirl** the result when flames are blown skyward by spiraling winds; also known as a fire tornado

**flashy fuels** fuels that ignite easily due to their small surface area and dryness

**forward bursts** fast forward movements of a forest fire

**fuel** a substance that reacts to release lots of heat, usually by burning

**fuel load** an amount of fuel (usually wood) per area of land

**global warming** changes in the world's weather patterns caused by human activity

**GPS** stands for Global Positioning System, a navigation system that uses satellites to pinpoint locations

**humid** a weather condition where there is a lot of moisture in the air

**infrared radiation** a type of invisible energy that is produced in large amounts when something is hot

**landslides** rock, mud, and debris that break off and slide down a slope

**monsoon** a seasonal wind that carries moist air inland in South and Southeast Asia, causing heavy rains

**pollution** something that adds dirty, harmful, or dangerous substances to air, water, soil, or space

**satellites** machines in space that can transmit signals to and from Earth

**sensor** a device that detects and measures

**surface area** the area of the outer part of something

# FOR MORE INFORMATION

## BOOKS

Rowell, Rebecca. *Wildfires* (Earth in Action). Minneapolis MN: Core Library, 2013.

Simon, Seymour. *Wildfires.* New York, NY: HarperCollins, 2016.

Thiessen, Mark. *Extreme Wildfire: Smoke Jumpers, High-Tech Gear, Survival Tactics, and the Extraordinary Science of Fire.* Washington, DC: National Geographic Children's Books, 2016.

## WEBSITES

Learn all about wild land fires, including campfire safety and information about what happens when forests do not burn naturally, at:
**smokeybear.com/en**

Watch National Geographic videos about forest fires at:
**video.nationalgeographic.com/search?q=forest+fire**

Explore the sections of a companion page for the NOVA movie, *Fire Wars*, with hotshots tackling a forest fire at:
**www.pbs.org/wgbh/nova/fire**

Check out some incredible pictures of forest fires and efforts to stop them at:
**www.wildlandfire.com/photos**

**Publisher's note to educators and parents:** Our editors have carefully reviewed these websites to ensure that they are suitable for students. Many websites change frequently, however, and we cannot guarantee that a site's future contents will continue to meet our high standards of quality and educational value. Be advised that students should be closely supervised whenever they access the Internet.

# INDEX

Africa 11, 14
air tankers 27, 30
animals 6, 11, 22, 24, 25, 32, 33, 35, 37, 45
ash 7, 9, 10, 20, 33, 36
Australia 14, 34–35, 37

bacteria 22, 25
benefits 36, 37, 45
Black Saturday Fire 34–35
bonfires 10
boreal forest 14
bushfires 4, 34

California 15, 24, 26–27, 44
campfires 4, 7, 11, 16, 17
causes of forest fires 9, 10–11
climate change 44
climates 4, 15
coniferous trees 14, 18, 21, 39
controlled fires 35, 37, 38
crown fires 20, 31, 38

deciduous trees 14, 15, 18
drones 30, 43
drought 12, 17, 26, 34, 44

Europe 14

fire line 28
fire retardant 30, 31, 33
fire spotting 20, 27, 42, 43
fire whirls 16, 17, 27
fireballs 20, 21, 34
firebreak 28, 30, 35, 38, 39
firefighters 6, 8, 13, 27, 28–29, 30, 31, 32, 35, 38, 39, 41
flames 4, 6, 7, 8, 9, 10, 13, 16, 17, 19, 20, 21, 22, 23, 24, 27, 28, 30, 32, 35, 39, 41
flash point 9
fuel 8, 9, 14, 16, 17, 18–19, 20, 23, 24, 27, 28, 37, 38, 39, 44
fuel load 19, 23, 27, 28, 38, 39, 44

global warming 44, 45

heat 4, 6, 8, 9, 10, 12, 15, 16, 18, 19, 20, 24, 25, 28, 29, 34, 36, 37, 42, 43, 44, 45

India 15
Indonesia 11, 25

lightning 9, 10

Malaysia 11
Mediterranean forest 14

oxygen 8, 9, 16, 28, 30, 41

peat 4, 19
preventing fire 38–39, 44, 45

rain 14, 15, 17, 25, 26, 33
rainforests 11, 15
Russia 7, 12–13

signs 20, 42
Singapore 11
slash-and-burn farming 11
smoke 7, 11, 12, 13, 17, 20, 22, 23, 24, 26, 27, 29, 31, 35, 42
smoke jumpers 31
soil 4, 19, 25, 36, 38, 45
South America 14
Southeast Asia 14
sparks 6, 10, 11, 34

temperate forest 14
tropical forest 14

United States 14, 40

volcanoes 10

warnings 20, 40, 42–43
wildfires 4, 23, 26, 27, 29, 30
wind 6, 12, 14, 15, 16, 19, 20, 26, 27, 31, 33, 34, 35, 40, 44
woodlands 4, 5, 11, 12, 25, 42